THE IN-CROWD

PATRICIA REILLY

LEVEL 2

SCHOLASTIC

'The In-Crowd' written by: Patricia Reilly

Fact Files written by: Jacquie Bloese, Sarah Johnson

Commissioning Editor: Jacquie Bloese

Editor: Fiona Beddall

Cover design: Ian Butterworth, Emily Spencer

Designer: Dawn Wilson

Illustrator: Stephen Elford

Picture research: Emma Bree

Photo credits: Cover: Imagesource; L. Adamski-Peek/Stone/Getty Images. **Pages 4 & 5:** Stockbyte; Imagesource; Brand X; P. S. OCarroll/Photo Alto; Photodisc. **Page 39:** Hemera; LTB. **Pages 42 & 43:** J. Wiedel, Popperfoto/Alamy; D. Cheskin/PA/Empics; Hemera. **Pages 44 & 45:** S. Botterill, P. Barker, B. Radford/Getty Images.

The publishers would like to acknowledge the following teachers for reporting on the manuscript:

Carine Chaput, Collège Ozar Hatorah, Toulouse, France

Kleio Drosou, Vytina High School, Arcadia, Greece

Beata Eigner, GRG, Vienna, Austria

Marie-Christine Jacquot, Collège Saint-Maimboeuf, Montbeliard, France

Adele James, Nea Paideia, Hydrari, Greece

Brigitte Neustifter, SHS Weiz, Weiz, Austria

Gertraud Noeth, Christian-von-Bomhard Schule, Uffenheim, Germany

Theodora Papavasiliou, English Language Centre, Trikala, Greece

Monique Peubez, Institution des Chartreux, Lyon, France

Maria Santoliquido, IPSCP 'Marcello Dudovich', Milan, Italy

Mary Glasgow Magazines (Scholastic Inc.)
Commonwealth House
1–19 New Oxford Street
London WC1A 1NU

Printed in Italy.

CONTENTS

THE IN-CROWD

Cameron McKenzie

Cameron is 15 years old. Until last month he lived in Scotland, but he and his family have now moved to Manchester. He liked his Scottish school, and he liked being captain of the school football team. He doesn't want to start again at a new school.

Shona McKenzie

Shona is Cameron's sister. She's 14 years old. She's much better than her brother at making new friends.

The In-Crowd

These are the coolest, best-looking students at school. Everyone wants to be friends with the in-crowd.

Jack: leader of the in-crowd and captain of the football team

Jenny: Jack's sister

Justin and Matt: Jack's best friends

Victor Mortimore & Marina Newsome

Victor and Marina are in Cameron's class at his new school. They are both interested in drama.

THE IN-CROWD

CHAPTER 1 A NEW SCHOOL

Cameron McKenzie sat on his bed and looked at his new school clothes. With his red hair, the red jacket looked terrible. It wasn't fair. Today was his first day at an English school. England! His friend Iain was always telling jokes about the English and now he was living there.

He didn't know anything about the move to England a month ago. Then one day his mother said, 'Shona, Cameron, we've got some news.' She smiled. 'You're dad's got a new job! In Manchester.'

His sister Shona said excitedly, 'Manchester? Fantastic – it's got some really cool clubs!'

His mum laughed.

'But I don't want to leave Scotland!' Cameron said.

'Please try to understand, love. It's important for your dad.'

And three weeks later they moved.

•••

Cameron really didn't want to start school in Year 10. 'They've all been there for three years, so they've already made friends,' he thought. 'I bet it's horrible … not like Scotland. *And* the school's probably got a terrible football team.' Cameron loved football. He was very short for his age, but in football that wasn't important. Secretly he planned to play for his favourite team, Celtic, one day. He kicked his school bag. No friends, no football and a stupid English school.

Cameron walked into the kitchen. Shona smiled at him.

'Hey, big brother, don't worry. It'll be OK!'

'I'll be in the car,' he said. Shona was only trying to help He knew that. But he didn't want to talk to her. 'It's OK for Shona,' he thought. 'She loves meeting new people and doing new things. She'll soon make some English friends.'

Cameron's mum drove them to their new school, Didsbury Manor. 'Enjoy your day,' she said. They got out of the car and walked into school. Cameron was behind a tall good-looking boy and pretty blonde girl when they suddenly stopped. Cameron crashed into the boy.

'Hey, you, be careful!' the boy said angrily.

'But … but it was an accident,' Cameron started to say. But the boy wasn't listening. He turned to his girlfriend and said something. They both looked at Cameron and laughed.

'Forget it, Cam,' Shona said. 'See you later.'

•••

Cameron finally found his classroom. There was a group of about ten students in the centre of the room. The good-looking boy and his girlfriend were in the group. They were all talking and laughing loudly together.

'Hi, Ellen. Wow, you're really brown!'

'Yeah, we went to Ibiza. It was fantastic. We went to a different club every night. The clubs are, like, really cool!

Anyway, I met this Spanish boy … It was great fun. What about you?'

'Jack, how are things? You've got a piercing! That's so cool.'

'Hey, Justin! How was Florida?'

'Florida? It was OK, I guess.'

Cameron looked at the group of students. They all seemed happy and popular. He wanted to be more like them. 'I bet they have a lot of fun. I'd love to be friends with them,' he thought.

Some of the other students were looking at the group too. Others sat in pairs and talked quietly. Suddenly he heard a voice behind him.

'Hi, there! Good holiday?'

'I went walking in the mountains with some friends …' But the boy wasn't talking to him – he was talking to one of the girls in the group! The group stopped talking and they all looked at Cameron.

'Matt! Hello … Yeah, good. And you? I bet you didn't go walking in the mountains!' Ellen said. She smiled at Matt.

Just then a teacher walked in.

'Right, everyone. Sit down. I'm Mr Grant and I'm your class teacher this year.' He stopped. 'Jack Sullivan, is that a piercing? Take it out. This is a classroom, not a fashion magazine. You can't wear piercings here – you know that.'

The class laughed.

'Now, we have a new student this year, Cameron McKenzie. Cameron's just moved here from Scotland …'

Cameron didn't hear the rest. Everyone was looking at him and his face was going red. He looked down at the desk while Mr Grant told them about their lessons for the year.

•••

'Right, time for lunch. Don't forget that homework for Friday,' the French teacher said. Everyone started to leave the classroom. Cameron looked up. Two boys were looking at him. He remembered their names: Justin and Matt.

'Er, where do we go for lunch?' he asked.

'Are you from Scotland, then?' Matt said.

'Aye, from Saint Andrews.'

'I from Saint Andrews?' Justin said. 'It's *I am*, you know. *I am from Saint Andrews*. Does no one teach you to speak correctly in Scotland, then?'

'No, not *I – aye*. A-Y-E. It means *yes*,' Cameron said.

'Aye, aye,' Justin and Matt said a few times. They laughed and then walked out.

Cameron put his books in his bag and slowly followed them. They were probably going to lunch. He was right. He got some food and sat down at an empty table. Two girls and a boy sat down at the other end of the table. Justin and Matt were sitting at the next table with a few other students.

Suddenly, Justin said loudly, 'Cameron's a girl's name, you know. Like that one in the films, Cameron Diaz …' Matt and Justin both laughed.

'But she's much better-looking. And she's taller!' They laughed again.

Cameron finished eating. For the rest of the lunch hour he read a sports magazine. There was a story about his old football team.

'That's impossible now,' Cameron thought unhappily.

•••

The afternoon classes seemed really long, but finally the last lesson finished.

'See you tomorrow.'

'Yeah, see you later.'

'Phone me tonight, then.'

'Bye.'

Everyone was talking to someone – except Cameron. He put his things in his bag and walked out.

Shona was waiting for him outside. She was in the centre of a group of students and they were all laughing.

'Hey, Cam,' she said, 'the English are good fun!' Everyone laughed – except Cameron.

'I want to be back in Scotland,' he thought.

CHAPTER 2 NEW FRIENDS

Next morning, Cameron arrived at school early. He was sitting at his desk when a bag hit him in the back. It was Justin's.

'Oh, sorry … who's that? Oh, it's the little Scottish boy! He's so small, I didn't see him there,' he said.

'But with that red hair, it's difficult *not* to see him!' his friend Matt said. They both laughed.

'Hey, Cameron!' It was the boy from his table at lunch yesterday. He seemed friendly. 'Don't listen to those two. They think they're cool. But people only talk to them because they're friends with Jack and the others.'

'Er, who's Jack?'

'He's the captain of the football team and he's, like, the leader of the in-crowd …' the boy answered.

'The in-crowd?'

'Yeah, you know, the popular group. They always wear cool clothes and go to the coolest parties. Well, they think they do!'

'Oh, right. And did you say that he's the captain of the football team?' Cameron asked.

'Yeah. That's him.' The boy pointed at someone.

'Oh, no!' thought Cameron. 'I crashed into him yesterday – the leader of the in-crowd …'

'Anyway, I'm Victor.' He smiled. 'Do you like football, then?'

'Yeah, I was captain of the team at my old school,' said Cameron. 'What about you?'

'Me? No way!' Victor laughed. 'I haven't got time for football. I'm in the drama group and we're doing *Romeo and Juliet*. We started working on it in the last week of the holidays, and we have two or three rehearsals every week.

Hey, do you know about the trials for the football team? They're on Thursday after school. I'll show you the sports notice board later. You have to write your name on the board.'

'I'm not sure …' Cameron started to say, but the English teacher walked in and the first lesson started.

•••

It was break time.

'Hey, Victor, how're you doing?'

'Hello, Marina. I'm just going to show Cameron the notice board.'

'I'll come with you,' Marina said.

'Marina's in *Romeo and Juliet* too,' said Victor. 'She's playing Juliet. She's really good – but not as good as Romeo.'

Marina laughed. 'And who's Romeo, Cameron? I bet you can't guess …'

'Umm … is it Victor, perhaps?' said Cameron. He looked at Marina and she smiled. She had lovely eyes.

There were three big notice boards near the school entrance.

'That's the sports board.' Victor pointed to the board at the end. Victor and Marina went to the drama board. They wanted to find out about their next rehearsal. Cameron walked over to the sports board and read: 'Team trials: Thursday 4.30 p.m.'

He wasn't sure about the trials. 'OK, I'll write my name,' he thought. 'It doesn't mean that I have to go to them.'

Then he heard voices. He looked around. Jack, Justin and Matt were walking to the notice board. Cameron wanted to escape as fast as possible.

'Look!' Matt said. 'I don't believe it! Little Scotty thinks he can get into the football team!'

'Maybe he's planning to run between the other players' legs!' Justin said. 'I'm certainly going to watch the trials. They'll be really funny!'

'Well, Jus,' said Jack, 'it's good that you'll be busy during the trials. We certainly don't want you to *play* in them.' Matt laughed and Justin looked angry.

'Get lost, Jack,' he said.

'Where do you play?' Jack asked.

'Midfield,' said Cameron.

'Oh, we need some good midfielders. Well, I'll see you there,' Jack said. He left with Matt.

'Football's a dangerous game,' said Justin angrily. 'Be careful. You don't want to have an accident!'

Victor and Marina came and joined Cameron. There was another girl with them.

'This is Kate,' Marina said. 'She's …'

'Not in the drama group,' Kate said. 'And that means that *I'm* normal,' she laughed.

'Your name isn't on the board,' Victor said to Cameron. 'You have to write it on before the end of school today, you know.'

'Erm … I'm not sure that I want to be in the team,' Cameron said. 'I'll think about it.'

The others looked at him, but nobody said anything.

'Come on, let's go. It's nearly time for class,' Marina said finally.

'I want to speak to Mark,' Victor said. 'See you in class.'

•••

After two boring lessons, Cameron walked slowly down to lunch. He couldn't decide about the team trials. He wanted to be in the football team, but he didn't want to have problems with Justin and his friends. He got his lunch and sat down on the same table as Kate and Marina.

'Victor says you were the captain of the football team at your old school,' Kate started.

'You have to go to the trials!' Marina said.

'Yeah, don't worry about Jack and his friends,' Kate laughed. 'Justin scored a … what do you call it? An own goal? You know, when you put the ball in your own team's goal. Anyway, my brother says Jack was really angry.'

They all laughed and Cameron started to feel better. 'I'll write my name on the board after lunch,' he thought.

They finished lunch and Kate and Marina went for a walk outside. Cameron went back to the sports board. But the piece of paper with the names for the trials wasn't there!

'Oh no! What am I going to do?' he thought.

Victor arrived. 'Are you looking for the team trials names?' he said. He looked very happy. 'Mr Tucker, the sports teacher, took the names away before lunch.'

'Yes, and my name isn't there,' said Cameron.

'Oh yes, it is.'

'No, it isn't.'

'It is. I saw it,' said Victor.

'I don't understand,' Cameron said.

'*I* wrote it, stupid!' Victor said. 'I found out from Mark that Mr Tucker usually takes the names away before lunch.

So I wrote your name on the board for you.'

'Great!' said Cameron. 'Thanks, Victor.'

'No problem,' he answered.

•••

Cameron walked out of school with Marina and Victor. Shona was waiting for him.

'Hey, how's it going?' she smiled.

'Oh, this is my sister. This is Marina and Victor.'

'Hi. I'm Shona.'

'Right, guys – see you tomorrow,' Marina said. 'Bye, Shona.'

'OK. Bye then,' Cameron said.

'Bye.'

CHAPTER 3 THE TEAM TRIALS

Cameron's mouth was dry. He looked at his watch for the fourth time. Mr Tucker was two minutes late.

Finally Mr Tucker arrived. 'Right, let's see some football. You six can play on Brian's team.' He pointed to a group of boys. 'The rest of you can play on Jack's team.'

Cameron was on Jack's team.

'Sam, you're our striker,' Jack said. 'Let's have some goals! The rest of you, play in midfield. I'll defend.'

The game started. After a few minutes Cameron stopped worrying and started to enjoy the game. He made some good passes. It was great to play football again. He was running up the field when one of the players in Brian's team kicked the ball badly. Luckily, Cameron was able to reach it.

'Hey, over here!' It was Sam and no one was defending him. Cameron just needed to pass the ball to him and Sam could score. It was difficult, but he decided to try. His foot touched the ball and he knew – it was a great kick. Yes! The ball was going to Sam. A few seconds later Sam scored.

After about half an hour, Mr Tucker said, 'Right, OK. That's enough for today. I'll put the names for the team on the board tomorrow morning. Thanks for coming.'

Cameron was going to the changing room when Mr Tucker called, 'McKenzie! Can you come here for a minute?'

Cameron walked over to him.

'You're new, right?' said Mr Tucker.

'Yes,' answered Cameron.

'Did you play for a team at your old school?'

'Yes, I did. Um … I was captain of the team last year.'

'OK. Well, you're in the team. Team practice is on Mondays after school, OK?'

'Aye … I mean yes … I mean great!'

He walked into the changing room. 'I'm in the team,' he thought. 'I've got some new friends and I'm in the team!' He was really happy. Then he heard some voices.

'Did you see that new guy?'

'Yeah. He only passed the ball to Sam because he can't score goals himself.'

'But I bet he's in the team. Tucker's talking to him now.'

'Yeah? Well, I won't pass the ball to him.'

'No, I won't either.'

Cameron put on his clothes sadly. It wasn't fair.

The next day he told Victor and Marina about the trials. 'Mr Tucker says that I'm in the team!' he said.

'That's great news!'

'Hey, you.' It was Jack. Justin and Matt and some of their group were with him.

'Er, hi Jack,' Cameron said.

'We've got a match at lunchtime on Friday. It's just a friendly game, but it'll be good practice for us. Don't forget.' He went back to his girlfriend.

Justin came over to him. 'You think you're so great, just because you're in the team. Well, maybe you won't be in it for many matches ...'

'Come on, Jus. We're going to check our emails in the computer room. Are you coming?' Matt shouted. Justin left.

'Forget him.' Marina said.

'Don't worry about it,' Victor agreed.

'I just want Justin to leave me alone,' Cameron thought, but he didn't say anything.

•••

On Friday, Victor, Marina and Kate watched the match. The first half was terrible. Cameron got the ball and passed it lots of time. But nobody passed to him. Twice he was near the goal with no defenders near him, but no one on his own team gave him the ball. Instead, one of the strikers, Oliver, tried to score, but he missed the goal both times.

When the first half finished, Mr Tucker called the team for a talk.

'What are you all doing? Have none of you got eyes in your heads?! Twice McKenzie was ready to score a goal, but nobody passed to him.' Mr Tucker wasn't happy. 'McKenzie is passing the ball well, but he's the only one. You're a team, remember. I want to see some teamwork and some goals!'

Nobody said anything, but Cameron could feel all their eyes on him. 'I want to be back in Scotland,' he thought.

His team scored one goal in the second half, but they lost the match 2–1.

After the match he joined his friends.

'I don't understand,' Kate said. 'Why didn't they pass the ball to you?'

'Yeah, you were right by the goal,' Victor agreed.

'They don't want to play with me,' Cameron said.

'Well, you played really well anyway,' Marina told him. She smiled.

'She's really nice,' Cameron thought. 'But does she like Victor? They spend a lot of time together. Maybe she's his girlfriend.'

He was still thinking about Marina when Oliver, the striker, walked past them with another guy in the team.

'That McKenzie's impossible,' said Oliver. 'Just because Tucker likes him, he thinks he's David Beckham!'

'He didn't miss two goals like you,' Marina said loudly.

Oliver turned to Marina, but his friend said, 'Leave her. She's only a girl. What does she know about football?!' They laughed and walked away.

A few weeks later, after class, Victor phoned Cameron.

'What are you doing on Saturday night?'

'Nothing special. Why?' asked Cameron.

'I'm meeting my girlfriend and some of her friends. Do you want to come?'

'Your girlfriend?'

'Yeah, Carly,' said Victor. 'She goes to another school but she lives near me. You'll like her.'

'You're not, er, going out with Marina, then?'

'Marina? No, she's just a friend. She likes drama, so we see each other a lot. But she's not my girlfriend.'

Suddenly Victor said, 'Hey! You like Marina!'

'Er …'

'Why don't you invite her too?' Victor said.

'Um, well, *I'll* come,' Cameron said. 'And *maybe* I'll ask Marina.'

'We can meet at my house first,' Victor said. 'See you tomorrow.'

'OK, bye.'

CHAPTER 4 THE MATCH

On Monday morning Cameron met Victor as he was walking into school.

'Hi Cameron, how's it going? Did you enjoy Saturday?' Victor asked.

'Yeah, I really liked the film. And your girlfriend Carly seemed nice.'

'Why didn't you ask Marina?'

'Well, I , er … maybe next time.'

'So, when's the big match? Is it this week?' Victor asked.

'Yeah, on Friday. And it's a really important game. We've got to win it or we're out of the cup! *And* we're playing Park School. They won last year, and the year before, and the year before that …' Cameron said.

'Look, don't worry. The team's much better than last year – *you're* in it! Hey, I've got an idea. Let's go out on Friday night – a big night out after your first big match. We can go to Patcha, that new club in town. They have an under 18s night on Fridays. Carly wants to go and I can ask Marina.'

Cameron smiled. 'Great!'

'OK, I'll ask the girls,' said Victor.

•••

The week passed really slowly. Cameron couldn't think about anything except the match. But Friday finally arrived.

'OK, this is an important match for us,' said Mr Tucker at the team talk. 'I know we can win. Just go out there and play your best football. Good luck!'

•••

There were only about fifteen minutes before the end of the match and Park School were leading 3–1. 'Park School are too good,' thought Cameron. 'We'll never win.'

Then Sam passed him the ball.

'I can score a goal from here,' he thought. 'It won't be easy, but I can do it. I know I can.' He kicked the ball.

'Goooooal!!!' the crowd shouted. The score was now 3–2, with twelve minutes before the end of the match. The ball went dangerously close to their own goal. 'Oh no!' thought Cameron. 'Are Park School going to score again?' But Jack defended well. He got the ball and passed to Cameron. Cameron looked around. Sam was free near the goal. He passed him the ball and Sam scored.

'Great goal!' Cameron shouted.

'Good pass, McKenzie!' Sam said. 'Come on, we're going to win this match!' Cameron felt wonderful. The score was now 3–3. Maybe they *could* win …

But five minutes later, it looked impossible again. The Park School defenders were playing brilliantly. No one could get the ball past them. Then suddenly Jack got the ball and started running with it. Cameron ran after him. They passed the ball between each other until they were almost in the goal area. Cameron had the ball when one of the defenders pulled his shirt. 'Penalty!' shouted everyone in the crowd.

Yes, it was a penalty. And it was the last minute of the match. They had to score.

'This one's yours, Cameron,' shouted Jack. 'You can do it!'

Cameron didn't hear the other guys in the team, or the excited crowd. In his head, everything was quiet. He looked at the ball, then at the goal. He ran … and kicked. It was just like in his dreams. He watched as the ball travelled slowly to the corner of the goal … as the goalkeeper tried to catch it … and as the ball went past the goalkeeper into the back of the goal!

Just then the match ended. They were the winners! 4–3 to Didsbury Manor!

Everyone in the team ran up to Cameron.

'We won! We won!'

'That penalty was brilliant!'

'Fantastic, McKenzie!'

It was almost like his old team.

Jack came up to him in the changing rooms. 'Hey, McKenzie, those two goals were beautiful. That penalty! You were great!'

'Thanks,' Cameron said in surprise.

'Beautiful, just beautiful,' Jack said. 'Right, I'm having a party at my house tonight. You've got to come. It starts about eight, OK?'

'Umm … can I bring some friends?' asked Cameron.

'Who? Not Victor and Marina?!'

'Yeah, and Victor's girlfriend …'

Jack stopped him. 'Listen, Cameron, no way! This is just *my* friends. Sam and Oliver from the team are coming. But

I don't want everyone there. Victor and Marina – well, they're just not cool, OK? Do you want to come or not?'

Cameron thought about it. He could be part of the in-crowd! He decided to go. 'I can meet Victor and Marina tomorrow night. They'll understand,' he thought.

'Yeah, thanks. I'll be there,' he said to Jack.

'Here's the address.' Jack gave him a piece of paper. 'See you there.'

Marina and Victor were waiting for him when he came out of the changing room.

'Brilliant match!' Victor said.

'You were great!' said Marina. 'And we're going to have a fantastic time tonight. Kate says Patcha's really cool.' She smiled at Cameron.

Cameron felt terrible. 'Listen … can we go tomorrow night? It's just that there's a … er … well … the thing is, everyone in the team is having a party. Yeah, there's a team party – you know, because we won the match.' He stopped. Victor and Marina looked upset.

'Oh,' Marina said. 'Tomorrow? I can't.'

'Well … you see … the team didn't want to speak to me before, and now …'

'Yeah, right. That's cool,' Victor said, but he didn't look very happy.

Cameron felt bad, but it was too late now. 'Look, I'll phone you tomorrow, OK?'

'Right, bye.'

'Bye.'

•••

Cameron had a great time at the party. Everyone was talking about his goals. A few times he thought, 'I'd like to be here with Victor and Marina.' But he went to bed happy. Now he was friends with the in-crowd.

CHAPTER 5 IN WITH THE IN-CROWD

'Hi, Cameron. How was your team party?' asked Marina on Monday morning.

'Oh … um … OK,' said Cameron.

'It's great that they're being friendly now.'

Victor came up to them. 'So how was Friday?' he asked. He didn't look very happy.

'Er, fine,' said Cameron.

Matt and Justin came into the classroom.

'Hey, McKenzie,' Matt said loudly. 'Did you enjoy yourself on Friday? Jack always has cool parties.'

'So, it's true,' Victor said. 'You went to Jack's party! Justin told me, but until now I didn't believe him.'

'What?' Marina said. 'It wasn't a party with the rest of the team?'

'Well,' Cameron said, 'Sam and Oliver were there. I thought Jack was inviting all of the team … but …' He went red. He wasn't very good at lying.

'Right,' Victor said. 'You prefer to spend your time with Jack and his crowd. You don't want to go to a club with us. That's fine. Just don't lie about it.'

'But I thought it *was* with the team!' Cameron said again. 'Really.'

Marina looked at Cameron. Then she went and sat at her desk.

'Victor, it was a mistake,' said Cameron.

Victor said, 'Yeah, right. It's OK.'

Cameron looked up and saw Justin. Justin was smiling, but it wasn't a nice smile.

•••

Cameron walked down to lunch alone. He was waiting for his lunch when the two boys behind started pushing him. They were in one of the other classes in Year 10, but Cameron didn't know them.

'Move, Shorty!' one of them said.

Suddenly, Jack walked up to them. 'Hey, you two! Don't talk like that. This is McKenzie. He scored two goals against Park School!'

'Hey, *you're* McKenzie?'

'Yeah, he is. So leave him alone!' Jack laughed.

'Right, McKenzie. See you, then,' the first boy said.

Cameron felt two metres tall!

•••

Cameron and Jack got their lunch together and then walked over to Jack's usual table. Most of the in-crowd were already there.

'Move along a bit!' Jack said. 'Great footballers need to eat!' They all laughed. They were still sitting at the table when Victor and Marina came into the dining room. Victor came over.

'Hey, Cameron, do you want to go out this Saturday?' he smiled.

'Get lost, Mortimore!' Matt laughed. 'He's coming out with us on Saturday. Right, McKenzie?'

'Um …' Cameron said. He wanted to go out with Victor and Marina, but he wanted to go out with Jack too. People wanted to be his friend when he was with Jack.

'Cameron?' Victor asked.

'Look, maybe another day,' he answered finally.

Victor walked away.

'Where are we going on Saturday?' he asked Matt.

'Patcha. It's this really cool club in town. I bet Victor doesn't know it. They don't let uncool people like him through the door!' They all laughed. Cameron laughed too, but he felt bad. He wanted to say something to Matt, but he didn't want them to laugh at him.

•••

He didn't see much of Marina and Victor that week. He told himself that they were just busy with rehearsals. But really he knew that they weren't busy *all* the time.

But now, suddenly, the other students in his year started speaking to him. They all talked about the match.

'Fantastic goals!'

'How did you feel before the penalty?'

'We're going to win the cup this year, McKenzie!'

He had lunch with Jack and the others every day and they made plans for Saturday evening.

'We're all going. It's a really cool club and there'll be lots of good-looking girls,' Matt said. 'Have you got a girlfriend?'

'No,' Cameron said. He thought about Marina.

'Well, I bet you meet someone on Saturday. Girls love footballers!'

'Aye,' said Cameron, but he didn't laugh.

•••

When Cameron arrived at the club he didn't feel very comfortable. It was his first time in a club like this. Then he saw Marina. She was dancing with Kate and she looked really good. He smiled. Marina saw him and smiled too. He was walking up to her when Jack arrived with a girl.

'McKenzie, this is my sister, Jenny. She's in Year 9,' Jack shouted. Jenny smiled at him. What could Cameron do? Marina was waiting for him, but he couldn't just leave Jack and his sister. When he didn't come over, Marina looked really upset.

'Jack's told me about you,' Jenny said.

'Um ... hi,' Cameron answered. He wasn't very good at talking to girls. The music was really loud and it was difficult to hear anyone anyway. Then Jack shouted, 'Why don't you ask my sister to dance? She likes you!'

'Oh ... um ... OK,' Cameron said. He didn't really want to dance with Jenny, but he didn't want to upset Jack either. Soon Cameron and Jenny were dancing. Cameron didn't know the song and he wasn't enjoying himself.

'Cool song,' Jenny shouted.

'Yeah,' he answered.

'Cool place,' she said.

'Yeah.'

'And you're cool too!' she said.

'Doesn't she know any words except *cool*?' Cameron thought. The song finished and he saw Marina again. 'I'll be back in a minute,' he said to Jenny. She looked at him and then she looked at Marina.

'Why do you want to talk to *her*?' Jenny said. She looked angry. Then she held his face in her hands and kissed him.

'Hey, stop it!' said Cameron. But it was too late. He saw Marina and Kate. They were leaving the dance floor. Kate had her arm around Marina.

Cameron didn't enjoy the rest of the evening. He wanted to talk to Marina, but he couldn't see her. It was almost impossible to have a conversation with Jenny because she was so boring. But Jack and the others left Cameron and Jenny alone together. Did they think that he was interested in her?

'Hey, McKenzie, be nice to my sister – I'm watching you!' Jack joked at the end of the evening.

CHAPTER 6 STRANGE MESSAGES

'How was the club?' Shona asked the next morning.

'Boring,' Cameron answered.

'Were Marina and Victor there?'

'Victor wasn't, but Marina was there with Kate.'

'So why was it boring? I thought you liked Marina. Did you dance with her?'

'I was with Jack and his sister. I didn't talk to anyone else. I'm, um … well, the thing is, I'm not exactly speaking to Marina and Victor at the moment. Because of Jack's party … and well … I'm really busy with football and things …' Cameron said.

'But Marina and Victor are really nice! Jack and his friends are only interested in you because you're good at football.'

'Shona's right,' he thought. He decided to speak to Marina and Victor the next day and say sorry.

•••

On Monday morning, he felt a bit better. He always had fun with Victor and Marina. He didn't have to be cool when he was with them. He could just be himself. 'I'll say sorry and then we can all be friends again,' he thought.

He saw Marina and Kate. They were looking at a mobile phone.

'My grandparents gave it to me for my birthday,' Marina was saying.

'Wow,' said Kate. 'And it's got a camera too – fantastic!'

'Um … hi,' Cameron said. 'Marina, I …'

Kate looked at him angrily. 'We've got to go now,' she said. She pulled Marina away.

'Oh no,' Cameron thought. 'Well, maybe I'll speak to Victor first.'

He looked up. Jenny was looking at him and she didn't seem happy.

When break started he went over to Victor's desk. 'Er, Victor, can I speak to you?'

'What do you want?' Victor said. He didn't look very friendly.

'Look, I wanted to say … Well, I …'

'Your friends are waiting for you,' Victor said and pointed to Jack and Matt. They were standing at the door.

'Come on, McKenzie,' Jack shouted. 'We need to talk about the match tomorrow.'

'Well, you're clearly busy,' Victor said. 'Bye.' He left the classroom.

'This isn't going well,' Cameron thought. He felt a bit angry. He was trying to say sorry, but Victor and Marina didn't want to listen! 'I'll try again at lunchtime,' he decided. Then he joined Jack.

•••

He was walking to lunch when he got a text message on his mobile.

SAW U WITH YR NEW GIRLFRIEND ON SAT.
B CAREFUL! SHE'S JACK'S SIS

'Saw you with your new girlfriend on Saturday. Be careful! She's Jack's sister,' he read. What did it mean? And who was it from? He tried to find the sender's number, but he couldn't. It was probably Justin or Matt. They liked this kind of joke.

He couldn't see Marina or Victor in the dining room. They were probably at a rehearsal.

He was eating his lunch when he got another message on his mobile.

STAY AWAY FROM HER!

'Her? Stay away from who? From Jenny? Or who? And who sent it?' thought Cameron.

A few seconds later, he got a third text message.

JULIET LOVES ROMEO, NOT U.

He thought about the message. Maybe it wasn't from Justin and Matt. 'Juliet loves Romeo.' Could it be from Marina? She had a new phone. Was she sending him these strange messages because he spent Saturday night with Jenny?

'Hi, Cameron.' It was Jenny. 'What's wrong?' she asked. 'You don't look very happy.'

Cameron didn't really want to talk to Jenny. But these messages were really worrying him, and he wanted to talk to someone.

'I got some strange messages on my mobile,' he said. 'I think they're from Marina.'

'Oh, I saw her with Victor,' Jenny said. 'They looked very happy. They're going out with each other now.'

'Victor and Marina? No ... Victor's got a girlfriend, Carly. He really likes her,' Cameron said.

'Well, he seems to prefer Marina,' Jenny said. 'They wanted to keep it secret, but everybody knows.'

Suddenly Cameron wasn't sure. He didn't want to believe it, but maybe it was true. 'They never want to speak to me now,' he thought. 'Perhaps that's because they're going out with each other. I always thought they were more than just friends!'

•••

He was going into class when he got another message.

U THINK U R SO COOL.
WHO DO U THINK U R? LEAVE ME ALONE

'I've had enough of these messages!' he thought. He was angry now. He walked over to Marina and Victor.

'Look, I know all about you two!' he shouted. He turned to Marina. 'And I don't want any more of your messages!'

'Messages?' said Marina. She looked surprised. 'What messages?'

'On your stupid phone!' said Cameron.

'My phone? But it doesn't work yet, it …'

'Your new phone doesn't work? I don't believe *that*!'

'Cameron,' Victor said, 'Marina's phone hasn't got a SIM card. We're going to buy one after school.'

Cameron thought for a second. 'They both look very surprised. Maybe I'm wrong about them …' Then he remembered something. 'Of course! They're in the drama group. They're good at that kind of thing. They *are* lying.' And he walked away.

'Leave him,' Victor said to Marina as Cameron left. 'Forget it.'

He was still angry when he met Shona after school.

'Cam, I need to tell you something,' she said.

'And I need to tell *you* something. Marina and Victor! They …'

'Listen!' Shona said. 'It's about Marina, well, and about Victor too.'

'I know all about it!' Cameron shouted.

'Cam, just listen for a minute. Jenny sent you some text messages.'

'Jenny? No, it was Marina!' Cameron said.

'No, Cam. Jenny was telling a friend about it, and I

heard their conversation. She got your mobile number from Jack. She was careful that you couldn't find out the sender's number. Then you thought that the messages were from Marina. Jenny really laughed about that. She knows that you like Marina. She wants to make things difficult between the two of you, because *she* wants to go out with you.'

'Oh, no!' thought Cameron. 'Marina and Victor weren't lying. I was so stupid! What am I going to do now?'

CHAPTER 7 THE PARTY

The next morning, Cameron was having breakfast when his mum came into the kitchen.

'What do you want to do for your birthday, love?' she asked.

'He wants to have a party,' Shona said.

'A party?!' Cameron said.

'Yeah, and he'll invite some friends from school. Right, Cam?'

'I, er, yeah. Can I, Mum?'

'I'll have to talk to your dad but I'm sure he'll agree. It'll be nice to meet your friends.'

That evening Cameron's parents agreed to a party. Cameron could invite 15 friends, and Shona could ask a few of her friends, too. Cameron felt happy about the party for a few minutes, but then he started worrying.

'A party!' Cameron said when he and Shona were alone.

'Yeah. You can ask Jack and his boring friends – or not. But, more importantly, you can invite Victor and his girlfriend, and Kate and Marina. You can tell them about it tomorrow.'

'But maybe they won't want to come …' said Cameron.

He wasn't sure about this idea.

'Well, say that you won't have the party without them!'

'But they probably won't even listen to me,' he said. 'I didn't listen to *them* today.'

'Of course they'll listen,' Shona said.

It sounded very easy but Cameron wasn't so sure.

•••

'A party?' Jack said. 'Cool. Jenny likes parties … and other things!' he laughed.

'I can only invite 15 people so I'm not inviting Jenny.' Cameron didn't want to see Jenny after those stupid text messages.

'What?' said Jack. 'You're not inviting your girlfriend?!'

'Look, Jenny's not my girlfriend, OK!' said Cameron.

Jack didn't look happy.

'Only 15 people! That's not much of a party!' It was Justin.

'My parents don't want too much noise,' Cameron said.

'What? Are mummy and daddy going to be there too? Are we going to play children's games, then?' Matt joked.

'They'll be upstairs,' Cameron said. The others laughed.

•••

He invited some other people in the in-crowd. Then he talked to Victor. He told him all about the text messages.

'So, you see, Jenny sent the messages, not Marina,' he finished. 'And she told me that *you* were going out with Marina. I'm so sorry. I've been really stupid!'

'Forget it,' Victor said.

'Look, I'm having a party. Will you come? And Carly?'

Victor smiled. 'Try and stop me!' he said.

'Do you think Kate and Marina will come?' he asked.

Victor wasn't smiling now. 'I don't know, Cam. You'll have to ask them. Marina was really upset, you know.'

'I know – and it was all my fault.'

'Well ... it was Jenny's fault too,' Victor said.

•••

Cameron had to speak to Kate and Marina now. He felt worse than before an important football match. 'What am I going to say?' he thought.

When he found the two girls, he couldn't look at Marina. He looked at the floor and told them about the party.

'Saturday?' said Kate. 'We've already got plans. Right, Marina?'

Marina looked at Cameron as Cameron finally looked up. Their eyes met for just a second. Then Marina turned and walked away. She looked upset.

'I'm really sorry,' Cameron called after her. 'I was so stupid yesterday! You see, Jenny said ...'

Kate stopped him. 'Just leave Marina alone! She doesn't want to go to your party! I hope you and Jenny enjoy it!'

'I didn't invite Jenny,' Cameron said. 'I don't want her to come. I want you two to come.'

Kate looked surprised. She ran after Marina.

•••

It was Saturday night. Most people were already at the party, but Cameron didn't really want to speak to anyone.

'Cam, it's your party,' Shona laughed. 'Try to look a little bit happy!'

'Marina isn't coming,' he said.

'Really?' she said. 'Oh, I think she'll come.'

'She won't come. She hates me now,' Cameron said sadly.

Shona smiled. 'You'll see,' she said.

Cameron wasn't enjoying the party. It was his birthday, but nobody seemed to remember. Jack, Justin and Matt were talking together in a corner.

'Hey, can we have some better music?' Justin said. 'This is really boring.'

'Look, here's something good,' Matt said. He changed the CD and turned it on really loud.

Cameron turned the music down again. He didn't want everyone in Manchester to hear it.

'It *is* a party, you know,' Justin said.

'Is there any food?' Jack asked. He looked bored.

'Yeah, in the kitchen,' Cameron said.

They went to the kitchen and Cameron felt a bit better. But where were Victor and Carly? 'Perhaps they aren't coming,' he thought. Then he heard someone at the door. Maybe that was Victor. When he opened the door, he couldn't believe it. It was Victor and Carly … and Kate and Marina!

'Happy birthday to you,' they sang, *'Happy birthday to you, Happy birthday dear Cameron, Happy birthday to you!'* They were here!

'Come in,' said Cameron, 'before someone in the street hears you and calls the police!' They all laughed.

They came in and Victor gave him a present. 'It's from all of us,' he said.

Cameron opened the present. It was a book about famous footballers and a CD.

'So now you'll remember us when *you're* one of the famous footballers in the book!' Kate said and laughed.

'Wow, thanks! Let's go and listen to this CD.'

He went to the kitchen for some drinks. Jack, Justin and Matt were leaving.

'Come on, this is really boring. Let's go,' Justin was saying.

'Oh, are you going?' said Cameron. 'See you on Monday, then. Bye.'

He didn't care about the in-crowd. His real friends were here.

'Hey, Shona! Victor and Carly are here, and Kate and Marina too!'

'Great!' Shona said. 'But I'm not surprised. I told Kate and Marina about Jenny and her stupid text messages. They were really angry with her. Happy birthday, big brother!'

'Thanks, Shona,' said Cameron. He went back to the living room. Kate, Carly and Victor were talking together. Marina was waiting for him.

'So,' she said, 'are you having a nice birthday?'

Cameron looked at her. Her eyes really were lovely. They both smiled.

Too cool for

All schools have rules. Here are some of the most unpopular rules in UK schools.

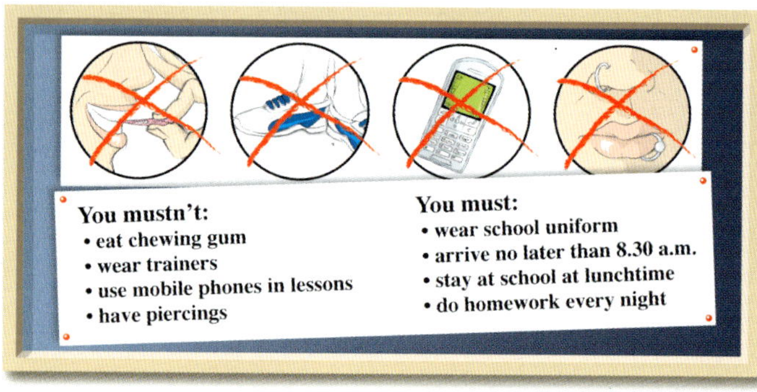

"You're in detention!"

If you break a rule, you sometimes have to stay after school 'in detention'. You have to sit in a classroom for 30 minutes and do boring schoolwork.

And when you get home after your detention, you then have to do your usual homework. Not cool!

Does your school have the same rules as UK schools?

Find these things in the pictures:
chewing gum uniform
school rules

school?!

Fun, fun, fun! **School life in the UK isn't only about rules, exams and homework. We asked some British teenagers their favourite things about school.**

" Every year at our school we have a talent show. It's a great laugh, and everyone enjoys it. You have to sing a song to everyone in the school. A group of teachers and students decides on the winner. Last year we did a song by Eminem. We didn't win. Everyone agreed – we were terrible! "
Ceri & Rob, 15, South Wales

Hampton Court

" I like it when we visit places outside school. Last summer we went to Hampton Court. King Henry VIII lived there more than 400 years ago. It was really cool! There were people in clothes from the 1500s. They showed us around the palace. And we had food from the time of Henry VIII in the kitchens at the end of the day. " **Janey, 14, London**

" At my school, we've got lots of sports clubs. In each sport, we play matches against other schools. I'm in the football club. We practise on Wednesdays after school and play a match every Saturday afternoon. "
Marcus, 14, Newcastle

What out-of-school activities do you do?

Find these things in the pictures:
talent show palace

Are you an

Do you want to be the same as everyone else in your class? Or do you think for yourself? Answer the questions and find out!

1 **Everyone in your class loves rap music but you hate it. What do you do?**

- ☐ **a.** You lie. You say that you love it.
- ☐ **b.** You talk about your favourite bands and singers.
- ☐ **c.** You tell everyone that you really hate rap.

2 **Your best friend wants to have a nose piercing. S/he says, 'Let's both have one.' You don't really like the idea. What do you say?**

- ☐ **a.** 'No way! I don't want to look like an animal!'
- ☐ **b.** 'OK – if you're going to have one.'
- ☐ **c.** 'I'm not sure. Will it hurt?'

3 **Josie is a new girl at your school. The in-crowd in your class don't like her and no one sits next to her. How do you feel?**

- ☐ **a.** You feel sorry for Josie but you don't often talk to her. You don't want to upset the in-crowd.
- ☐ **b.** You never think about Josie. If the in-crowd don't like her, you don't like her.
- ☐ **c.** You feel sorry for Josie and sometimes sit with her at lunchtime.

individual?

4 You find an old pair of purple jeans in your mum's cupboard. You really like them and wear them the next day. Your friends all laugh at you. What do you do?

- ☐ **a.** You lie. You say that you are wearing them as a joke. You don't really like them!
- ☐ **b.** You feel upset. Perhaps you won't wear them again.
- ☐ **c.** You tell your friends that you like them. You wear them when you go out the next time, too!

5 Your girl/boyfriend invites you to a party at a really cool club. But there'll be some horrible people from your school there. What do you say?

- ☐ **a.** 'Oh sorry ... er, I'm having dinner at my grandparents' house on Saturday.'
- ☐ **b.** 'Yeah, great! It'll be brilliant!'
- ☐ **c.** 'Forget it! I'm washing my hair on Saturday!!'

How many points did you get?

1 a = 1, b = 2, c = 3
2 a = 3, b = 1, c = 2
3 a = 2, b = 1, c = 3
4 a = 1, b = 2, c = 3
5 a = 2, b = 1, c = 3

0–5 points: Oh no! Do you have any ideas of your own? Don't always follow the crowd. You'll have more fun when you think for yourself!

6–10 points: Great. You can think for yourself when you want to. Remember – your friends aren't always right.

11–15 points: Brilliant! You have your own ideas and no one can change them. You are happy with your life and your friends. But be careful – let your friends have their own ideas too.

Scotland

What do you know about Scotland? It's time to decide: true or false?

'Scottish men wear kilts!'

True! Scottish men first wore kilts in the 1700s. The different tartans showed their different families or 'clans'. Today most

Scottish men have a kilt but they don't wear them every day. They only wear them at special times, for example at a party or special dinner.

'Scottish people don't speak English.'

False! All Scottish people speak English but there are two other Scottish languages – Gaelic and Scots. Only 60,000 people speak Gaelic, and very few young people speak it now. Almost all Scottish people speak Scots – a language like English but with a lot of special Scottish words.

'Scotland is the home of the Loch Ness monster.'

Who knows? Many people say they've seen the monster. There have even been some photos. But are the photos real? We

Which of these things started in Scotland?

TV

deep-fried Mars bar

whiskey

the telephone

penicillin

The answer is ... all of them!

can't be sure, because nobody has ever found proof of a monster. But Loch Ness is 44 kilometres long – the largest lake in Britain – and it's 230 metres at its deepest point. The water is very dark because it's so cold. Perhaps we'll never know its secrets.

Talk the talk

Here are some Scots words.

aye: yes

wee: small

bonny: pretty

a loch: a lake

a lassie: a girl

a ceilidh: (say 'caily') a party with dancing

Find these things in the pictures:

kilt lake monster tartan

FOOTBALL

Forget rugby and cricket – the number one sport in Britain is football!

When to watch:

• The English **football season** starts in August and finishes in May. Most matches are on Saturdays and start (or **kick off**) at three o'clock.

• If you can't go to a game, you can watch *Match of the Day* on television. This is one of the oldest football television shows – it started in 1964!

What to watch:

• In England, professional football is made up of four **leagues**. The top league is called the **Premiership**.

Thierry Henry

• There are twenty **teams** in the Premiership. The most famous and successful teams are Manchester United, Arsenal, Chelsea and Liverpool.

• Scotland has four, smaller leagues. The top league is called the **Scottish Premier League**, or **SPL**. The most famous Scottish teams are Celtic and Rangers. They are both from the same city, Glasgow, but they really hate each other.

Who to watch:

• The Premiership has got some of the best football players from all over the world: Ruud van Nistelrooy (Manchester United and Holland), Thierry Henry (Arsenal and France) and Cristiano Ronaldo (Portugal and Manchester United). But these days everybody is talking about an English player. His name? Wayne Rooney.

FRENZY

Name: Wayne Rooney
Nickname: Roo-naldo or Shrek
Team(s): Manchester United and England
Date of Birth: 24th October 1985

In September 2003, Wayne Rooney became England's youngest scorer in an international match. Wayne is also the most expensive teenager in the Premiership. He cost Manchester United £28 million.

How to score:

When someone asks you '**What's the score?**', remember this:

- 0 is not 'zero', but '**nil**'. For example: Manchester United 2 (two), Arsenal 0 (nil).
- If two teams have the same number of goals, it's a **draw**. If the score is 0–0 then it's 'nil–nil'. But for other numbers you say '**all**'. For example 2–2 is 'two all'.

How to buy a ticket:

- It's often difficult to buy a ticket for a Premiership match. Sometimes you have to wait six months for a ticket!
- Join the club of your favourite team first. You can do this on their website. Then it will be easier to get a ticket.

What to shout:

A British football match is noisy! To your own team you can shout or sing:

Come on you reds / blues!

When you're winning, you can shout or sing the score to the other team's fans.

Find this word in the pictures: fans

CHAPTERS 1–2

Before you read

1 Cameron loves playing football. Some of his friends love drama. Do you enjoy any out-of-school activities?

2 Match the two halves of these sentences about football.

a) He kicked	**i)** the ball.
b) He scored	**ii)** 3–0 after only five minutes.
c) They were leading	**iii)** a goal.

3 Which of these football nouns is NOT a person or people? You can use your dictionary.
a) goalkeeper **b)** crowd **c)** trials **d)** captain **e)** midfielder

4 Complete the sentences with these words. You can use your dictionary.
piercing **notice board** **rehearsal** **bet**
a) He's really good-looking. I ... lots of girls want to go out with him.
b) The drama group has a ... every Tuesday after school.
c) He's got a ... in his nose, and another above his right eye.
d) There's lots of information about out-of-school activities on the ... .

After you read

5 Answer the questions with the correct names.
Justin **Shona** **Marina** **Cameron** **Jack** **Victor**
a) Who is short with red hair?
b) Who is excited when his/her family moves to Manchester?
c) Who is the captain of the Didsbury Manor football team?
d) Who is in the drama group with Victor?
e) Who doesn't want Cameron to play in the team trials?
f) Who writes Cameron's name on the notice board?

6 What do you think?
a) Is Cameron going to go to the team trials?
b) Who are his friends going to be at the end of the story: the in-crowd, or Victor, Marina and Kate?

CHAPTERS 3–5

Before you read

7 What is the past simple of these irregular verbs?
a) make **b)** feel **c)** win **d)** hold

8 Complete the sentences. You can use your dictionary.
striker **defender** **passed** **missed** **kissed**
changing room **penalty**

- **a)** He's a ... because he's good at scoring goals.
- **b)** He ... the goal, so the score was still 0–0.
- **c)** He got a ... when a player on the other team kicked him in the head.
- **d)** He ... the ball to a player near the goal.
- **e)** The players got ready for the match in the ... .
- **f)** A ... tries to keep the ball away from his own team's goal.
- **g)** They were the cup winners again! Everyone in the team ... the cup for the cameras and the crowd shouted excitedly.

9 Guess the story. Choose the correct word in each sentence.

- **a)** Cameron **joins / doesn't join** the football team.
- **b)** The Didsbury Manor team **win / lose** an important match against Park School.
- **c)** Cameron goes to **Victor's / Jack's** party.
- **d)** **Marina / Jack's sister** kisses Cameron in a club.

Now read Chapters 3–5. Were your guesses right?

After you read

10 Are these sentences true or false? Correct the false sentences.

- **a)** Cameron scores a goal in the team trials.
- **b)** The other players don't want Cameron in the team at first.
- **c)** Cameron plays badly in the match against Park School.
- **d)** Cameron likes Jenny more than Marina.

11 What do you think?

- **a)** Cameron decided to go to Jack's party instead of the club with Victor and Marina. Did he do the right thing?
- **b)** Will Cameron have a girlfriend at the end of the story? Who?

CHAPTERS 6–7

Before you read

12 At the end of the story, Cameron has a party. What are the most important things for a good party?

13 Guess the story. Complete the sentences with the correct people.

Jenny **Shona** **Marina** **Jack** **Victor**

a) Cameron starts to think that Marina is going out with ... .
b) ... sends Cameron some text messages and tries to make trouble between him and Marina.
c) ... helps Cameron to be friends with Marina and Victor again.
d) ... doesn't enjoy Cameron's party.
e) Cameron is surprised but very happy when ... arrives at the party.

Now read Chapters 6–7. Were your guesses right?

After you read

14 Are these sentences true or false? Correct the false sentences.

a) Marina has a new mobile phone.
b) Cameron thinks that the strange text messages are from Marina.
c) Marina is now Victor's girlfriend.
d) Cameron shouts at Jenny about the text messages.
e) The birthday party is Shona's idea.
f) Cameron gets birthday presents from all the guests at his party.
g) Cameron is sad when the in-crowd leave his party early.
h) Marina comes to the party because Shona has told her about Jenny's text messages.

15 What do you think?

a) What will happen between Cameron and Marina?
b) Will Cameron and Jack be friends now?
c) Does every school have an in-crowd like the one in the story?
d) Is it easier to be popular if you are good at sport?